CONJUGATIONS
and REITERATIONS

ALSO BY ALBERT MURRAY

The Omni-Americans

South to a Very Old Place

The Hero and the Blues

Train Whistle Guitar

Stomping the Blues

Good Morning Blues:
The Autobiography of Count Basie
(as told to Albert Murray)

The Spyglass Tree

The Seven League Boots

The Blue Devils of Nada

Trading Twelves: The Selected Letters of Ralph
Ellison and Albert Murray
(edited by Albert Murray and John F. Callahan)

From the Briarpatch File

CONJUGATIONS
and REITERATIONS

ALBERT MURRAY

Pantheon Books   New York

TO MOZELLE AND MICHELE

All rights reserved under International and Pan-American Copyright Conventions. Published in the United States by Pantheon Books, a division of Random House, Inc., New York, and simultaneously in Canada by Random House of Canada Limited, Toronto.

Pantheon Books and colophon are registered trademarks of Random House, Inc.

"William Faulkner: Noun Place and Verb" originally appeared in slightly different form in *The New Republic.*

Library of Congress Cataloging-in-Publication Data

Murray, Albert.
Conjugations and reiterations / Albert Murray.

ISBN 0-375-42141-6 (alk. paper)
1. African Americans—Music—Poetry.   2. African Americans—Poetry.   3. Blues (Music)—Poetry.
4. Jazz—Poetry.   I. Title.
PS3563.U764 C66 2001   811'.54—dc21   2001031398

www.pantheonbooks.com

Book design by Johanna Roebas

Printed in the United States of America
First Edition
2 4 6 8 9 7 5 3 1

CONTENTS

I

Aubades
EPIC EXITS AND OTHER
TWELVE BAR RIFFS

early in the morning
  hear the rooster crow
early in the morning
  hear the rooster crow
hear the freight train coming
  whistle moaning low

old grandpa stole away
  north by freedom train
old grandpa snagged
  that underground freedom train
booked his passage through the grapevine
  stashed his pack
and prayed for rain, I mean heavy rain

once was the north star
    then it was the L and N
used to be the north star
    then it was the L and N
not talking about cincinnati
not telling nobody where or when

going down to the railroad
*   down to the railroad track*
going down to the railroad
*   down to the railroad track*
grab me an arm full of freight train
*   and ain't never ever coming back*

early in the morning
    hear the sawmill whistles blow
early in the morning
    hear the sawmill whistles blow
then when the school bells ring
    it's my time to be ready to go

they used to call me schoolboy
and I never did deny my name
when folks called me schoolboy
I never would deny my name
I said you've got to be a schoolboy
if preparation is your aim

early in the morning
   listening to the radio
early in the morning
   listening to the radio
first week on the campus
   four chime time years to go

I can drink muddy water
  sleep in a hollow log
yes, drink muddy water
  sleep in a hollow log
but one of these days
  I'll be back home walking the dog
along the avenue
  arm in cozy arm with you

I said what I said
*   and her smile said we shall see*
I said what I said
*   and her smile said we shall see*
ain't no line of jive gonna ever make a
*   fool of me*

get yourself together baby
  and let's get on some time
get yourself together baby
  and let's get on some time
this is the nitty gritty, baby
  this ain't no pantomime

some folks out here
trying to change things
some others just come
to have their say
some out here running risks
to change things
some others just saying
the same old say
takes more than huffing and puffing
to blow them jim crow blues away

found no enchanted castles
    so there were no magic keys
there were no enchanted castles
    and there were no magic keys
nor was there anyplace on this planet
    that was a realm of total ease

the world ain't promised me nothing
  so it don't owe me nothing at all
no, since the world ain't promised nothing
  it don't owe nobody nothing at all
makes no difference to the universe
  whether you walk, swim, fly or crawl

II

LANDSCAPE WITH
FIGURES

I

the thing about
scarecrow plug uglies
is that
everybody (and creature)
who does not ignore them in the first
    place
catches on to them sooner or later
indeed even before boogerbear-oriented
    children
grow up to construct fake monsters
of their own
there were already unimpressed crows
who had long since mistaken them for a
    perch
and endowed them with the patina
of public park monuments:
perhaps "three quarks for mr. marx"

---

but certainly "plip plop and spatter
    batter on you
mr. whoever or whatever the hell
you're supposed to be"

II

on the other hand
as municipal cleanup budgets
for red letter day celebrations
of legendary heroic actions
have always reflected
(no matter who is elected)
bird spatterings on the time-honored
stone, bronze or gold-gilded patina
of public monuments
are a serious matter
of respectful aesthetics
not just of vain
chamber of commerce cosmetics

mug ugly frogs
may sometimes be
princes in uncharming
disguise
the purpose of which
is to test
the future queen's
sense of ambiguity
remember, it's what
happened in the dark
that made the princess
light the candle

during an ivy league
pit stop:
overheard t.s. eliot
giving the lowdown
on the west forty
disguised as london town
fallen down
to the dongless ding
of the land of the fisher king!
wiping out the folklore
of white supremacy
with far more implications
immediate or long range
than jack johnson's jokey
demolishment of jack london's
ever so bright comeback hopes
for jim jeffries

the truth of fairy tales
　　must be read as formulas are
by substituting for the x, y, zero
　　situations of the hero
concrete details which represent
　　daily circumstances
thus are all romances
　　whether of people or of numbers
made to fulfill a social function
　　beyond mere elementary survival
and entertainment
　　ugly terrain and foul weather
(no less than fair)
　　come-hither castles,
cozy coves and reclining nudes
　　are required by narrative
as whatever is by mathematical convention
the dragons however in whichever image
　　or embodiment of entropy
are not only actual
　　but can wreak such devastation
as only combat experience
　　quod erat demonstrandum
can cope with
　　on the other hand
who knows how much luck (!) may always
　　be involved in the outcome of anything

24

to new york then I came
and found picasso's demoiselles uptown
in cotton club honey brown
projecting black and tan
(expense account) fantasy figures
replacing the can can
with the shuffle, the shimmy
and the birmingham break down

to the also and also
    of paris I also made my way
following jim europe's syncopated footsteps
    and those of louis and duke,
of both of whom the french said
    not what do they want
but what have they brought us this time

as for what I wanted:
    a rage of paris
publicity springboard
    to points thisaway
and thataway
    u.s.a.

but that was long ago
    when french word
was aesthetic law

one must measure
    one's own plurabilities
these days

III

FABLE IN THE FABRIC

if you got to ass
what it is
honey, you ain't yet with it,
thus old gates armstrong
(louis, yclept satchmo, erstwhile
satchel mouth and before that
dipper mouth, from which dipper & dip
even as satchmo was to become
satch
as in satchel foot for old satchel paige)

thus old satch (who was finally to become
     old pops)
to some fay chick unnamed
but variously quoted e.g. time, the
     newsmagazine
once the self-styled coca-cola of U.S.
     journalism:
2/21/49 "when you got to ask [sic!] what it is,

you never get to know"
and so old pops
had himself another glory
though some say it was also old fats
waller said it
who damn well could've
item: **man, if you don't know**
what it is
best you don't be trying
to mess around with it
so old fats too
whose eyes were forever saying
one never knows,
not do one?
but do one!

but questions pursue
the musicians backstage
as if verbalization means more than their
    music
indeed such used to be the downtown
    uproar
over duke's uptown downbeat
ass they did
and urgently, suspiciously
as if life itself were questionable
as if questions must always have answers

as if answers don't have questions of their
    own

as if facts beget experience
and information flesh and blood
so with as much cosmic implication
as is available to your own perception
of the nuts and bolts actuality
of anything whatsoever
you say—remembering bubba and duke:
it don't mean a thing
if it ain't got that swing
so do what? do art!
do what?
do art! do art!

nevertheless
the questions pursue the performer
not only backstage
but also back uptown (or crosstown, or
    wherever)
only to get the same answers
do art! do art! do art! do art!
do art! do art! do art! do art!
do what?
do art! do art! do art! do art!
do art! do art! do art! do art!

KC 4/4
(1)

said the nothing if not pragmatic
william james
basie,
the trigger-fingered count from
edmund wilson's red bank, new jersey,
by way of kansas city
and by virtue
of a not un-walt whitmanesque
four/four,
"beat, bite and real guts
under a good old post-ragtime
syncopated shout
with trumpet and/or trombone mutes
plungers and aluminum, plastic, felt
derby fans
will always put the blues
deep down in the dozens

talking about playing the dirty dozens with
    the devil!
(and if you don't play them
just pat your foot whilst I play them)
talking about how like the
oklahoma city
blue devils used to stomp
the red devils down in
slaughters hall and ralph ellison's other
deep second joints,
and remember
nothing is ever too slow
or too fast
to swing!"

KC 4/4
(II)

eventually
along with the already
universally irresistible kansas city four/four
came charlie parker
shouting the blues
that many bird intervals higher
and thus
with an even more captivating
velocity of celebration

PAS DE DEUX
(I)

all art,
said old walter pater,
speaking of sandro botticelli,
constantly aspires
toward the condition
of music.
so it is swing
that is the supreme fiction,
madam,
for
(given the concreteness
of physical experience *per se*)
our primary concern
is the quality of our consciousness
(how we *feel* about it all)
and swing, which is movement
and countermovement

which is life itself,
is that elegant resilience
that poetry would reenact,
its verbalization being
aesthetic kinetics!
after all, madam
(or rather first of all),
is not the primordial function
of verbal enchantment
the refinement
of our physical responses?
the objective of poetry
is to be *moving*, madam,
poetry is the supreme effort
to make words *swing*.
but, according to vico,
(giambattista, 1668–1744),
before articulation
became narration
there was only exclamation
(onomatopoeia)
along with pantomime
yes, as jamesjoyce came to know
and kennethburke came to say,
poetry is symbolic action
and symbolic action,

madam,
is the *dancing* of an attitude,
and dance, madam,
don't mean a thing
minus that insouciant element
of swing
there's your supreme fiction, madam,
it ain't what you do
it's the way that you do it.

l'envoie:
it must never
be more gymnastic
than elegant

II

swinging is never uptight,
my good fellow,
no sweat, my man,
cool, old pardner,
up-tempo relaxation
as it were, moreover,
given the inevitability
of entropy
and the ineluctable modality
of perception
and thus conception
swinging is not only
the most elegant mathematical
solution
it is also
the best revenge

Q & A

Do the mutes sublimate
underground grapevine whispers
do plungers compensate
childhood repressions
schoolyard frictions
or perhaps stool restrictions?

are juke joint piano sounds
your evocations of untold stories
of jim crow towns,
the black and white keyboard
suggesting segregation
your exclusion from paradise,
the black key minors
touched for tears?
not if they swing,
my man, miss lady,
not if they swing

IV

——⁂——

PROFILES

PREMIER CRU U.S.A.

american social science survey technicians,
whose *modus operandi* (nay, *sine qua*
    non!)
is segregation,
continue to proliferate norms and
    deviations
that are invariably skewed
to support the folklore of white supremacy
and the fakelore of black pathology
but the anecdotes
that most immigrants find most
    representative
are those horatioalgerisms that relate and
    reiterate
how the white human trash of europe
interacting with other human trash
of west africa and elsewhere

in accomplishing what the redskin elite
of the forest primeval had no aztec, inca,
    mayan
or toltec plans for
became the demographic cream of the
    crop
that by mid twentieth century
had already rendered the almanach de
    gotha
obsolete:
who is due at the castle
for dinner and global negotiations
bearing non-greek appropriations?

the progeny of all that
mayflower, middle passage and steerage
flotsam and jetsam
your highness
that's who.

PRIVATE STOCK

thelonious
the syncopating monk
whose preferred cloistersphere
seemed to be the misty morning
    atmosphere
of the after hours joint
from which the last of the nightlong
merrymakers have departed.
in all events
he almost always used to seem
to be resampling his honky-tonk piano
meditations and up-tempo stride time
    études
as much for his own private edification
as for the programmed entertainment
of any paying audience
indeed thelonious made music

as some monks have always made
and shared wine:
here's something else to my taste
try this
how about this
or
this

from washington
    once a man
and now a town
    came ellington
once a man
    and now a sound
that is storiella americana
    as she is swyung
up and down
    and all around
the globe

WILLIAM FAULKNER
NOUN PLACE AND VERB

memory he said believes he said
and himself did who was himself
memory and did himself believe
and then remember to recollect,
whose name was william faulkner
whose place was mississippi
and whose verb was tell.

memory he wrote believes before knowing
remembers. believes longer than recollects
longer than knowing even wonders
knows remembers believes, he himself said
believing himself and mississippi august
    skylight
mississippi thickets in september
    twilight,
believing the dry hysteria: *something*

is going to happen I am going to do
  something
something is going to happen to me

and memory no less in mississippi than
  elsewhere
believes knows tells this:
the mississippiness of ancient oracles
of albatross sins ancestral; recollects
  remembers this:
presummersmell of wisteria
oldentime ladies in rooms unsanctuary
amid mississippi gothic behind cottonwhite
totems doric corinthian scotch irish
(O clytemnestra my black one
  O my firstborn son and brother)

and this also believes: cypress and gum trees
beach, cane and briar and three-note
  birdsong
reflections in branch water; mississippi
  distant horns
and gas engine smells fading beyond now
  and fury.
and this recollects and knows the
  significance of:

black human blood red on butcher knives
white female blood on phallic corncobs.

memory believing yoknapatawpha indian
    doom
did not mistake the wilderness for sanctuary
either but wished it so as huntsman
but wishing does not know
forgets and gallops confederate cavalry in
    gail (tone) hightower
sermons
wish-fulfilling knighthood (without negroes)
wish-forgiving arrogance and the outrage
    of human bondage
wish-denying antebellum insurrection
    nightmares
while celebrating those who could survive
    them
but wishing is believing too
because the bones remember
(O canaan look away from dixie
away from bedford forest O railroads
underground freedom bound)

and memory knowing this
knows more (believes infers

more complications than even those
miss rosa coldfield's perhaps once glittering
eyes gave quentin compson, who said:
and wants it told!)

memory
believes knows recollects in him *(whose*
    nouns
were courage and honor and pride and
he says pity and love and even justice
and liberty) believes knows and wonders at:
wishing become man-horse-demon
with twenty negroes (shackled) begetting
with one french architect (shanghaied)
    sutpens
hundred *(without gentleness begot,* miss
    rosa
coldfield says); wonders remembers
aghast but knows: mississippi dynasties
of somewhat
oedipal innocence with black
queen mothers and half brothers
knows jefferson the man and town
and public confederation of decorum; and
    also knows
remembers eighty miles to memphis

and miss reba's sanctum sanctorum of law
	and order
and sportsmanship

believes remembers
recollects, records in commissary ledgers
pharaoh-tale-accounts compounded in
	confounding
convolutions of all-too-human-impacted
good intentions which at any rate
reveal (or partly unconceal) himself:
william faulkner hamlet-hounded master
of mulatto metaphors among macbeths
in county courthouse castles out-
	demographed
by ever in-creeping miscegenated thickets

nigger? the sheriff said in hot pursuit
of the inherently illusive mississippi
	christmas,
nigger? he said. maybe nigger, maybe not
they told him then
whose memory like theirs believed in
	shadows
as much as men

INSIDE DOPESTER

sigmund freud, whose ego-id (or jekyll-
    hyde) dialectics
have become the opiate of so many
    contemporary U.S. intellectuals
to whom most dreams, however (whether
    pipe or utopian),
are not nearly so revolutionary as
    pornographic—
whose positive contribution to the mental
    health
of twentieth century mankind is not
    altogether
unquestionable, but who gave to gossip
    (back fence or cocktail party)
a terminological refinement it never had
    before,
did not write oedipus rex, antigone and
    electra

nor was he ever near colonus,
not circa 442 b.c. at any rate or sophocles
    who, incidentally,
not only made less insistent speculations
about bow and arrow wounds, for instance,
but also never forgot that dream oracles,
    like fortune tellers
are seldom scientific.

herr doktor (which is to say wish doctor)
    freud was the
father matriarch not of ancient greek
but of modern viennese mythology
he now rests, however, not in that city of
    elegant dressage
    (tho minus syncopating sidewalks!)
but in london the anglo-saxon citadel of
stiff upper lips
a refugee from the nastiness
of teutonic gas holes but not always
    consistently pro-semitic himself
resenting (somewhat) his own mostly nice
    paterfamilias
rationalizing it away with a cock and bull
    formula:
parental regard is to greek incest as filial
    disobedience

is to murder
and then charging his confused and
    scandalized patients
with (and for) hating (or loving) theirs
revealing in the process his other
    psychosis
as occupational: *the fee he said*
was part of the therapy

a natty dresser, a strict big daddy
who confessed moses but never met him
he could with impeccable-seeming
    manners
turn leonardo da vinci's dream kite into an
    italian vulture
and then proceed to desecrate the
    bloomers
of middle-aged nannies,
a long black non-viennese stogie
erect between his pale bearded lips the
    while
but, whether or not he shared jung's
naughty notions of U.S. negroes,
freud could never have forgiven their jazzy
    unconcern
with his own hopelessly unbooted
    conjectures

about mama love inhibitions and phallic
    envy.

all too sexual about matters intellectual
but always intellectual about matters sexual
the categorical professor freud became
downright academic
about such simple and completely ordinary
    things
as his and hers, and astonishingly
    theoretical
about what after all is the most natural
and necessary difference in the world.
and, what is more, remained all those years
adamant in his suspicion of fun
and games, preferring the dream world of
    fears,
queers, valse triste rituals, midnight tears.

and, almost as bad, his incurable
    freudianism
spoiled most jokes, and he decried most
    pranks
as intended crimes and seemed compelled
to make the simplest mistakes more
    embarrassing

by explaining them. but perhaps worst of
    all
he encouraged bookworms, statisticians
    and lab technicians
to assume that data can exorcise all
    adventure
and monographs expose the innermost
    secrets of wonderlands.

motivational revelations by all means
and the light which he gaveth shineth in
    the darkness,
yea verily, for thinking is indeed
mostly wishing—*tant pis (though perhaps*
    less often fish-wishy
than just plain wishy-washy)

but for all his carefully compiled dope
    sheets
he was not unlike so many cocksure
    tipsters
always somehow suddenly shy of the
    pragmatic
hands on, chips down
flags down, eggs down advice
poor old humpty dumpty's king's horsemen

need most urgently at post time
(it being too late for such freudulent
    hindsight
as: you should have stood longer in bed)
nor, come to think of it, did he ever really
convince himself or any of the faithful
that wishing won't wash any real enemies
    away.

nevertheless dear doctor freud, along with
    dear doctor marx,
remains the master of machine age
    medicine patents
most self-indulged by devoted disciples
but in them it all too often seems that he
    has bequeathed to posterity
more wise guys perhaps than wise men

POETA DE EPOCA
(1)

chez hemingway
the elemental is *per se*
and thus timeless
universal
indispensable
ergo his factuality and musicality
are inseparable
his conjugations therefore required
the cadence of process
become ritual
each episode being
a ceremonial reenactment
rendered on a rhetorical principle
preferring precision of syntax
to the elaboration of synonyms

$$(2)$$

sharks, he said,
do not share.
nor, he might have added,
do cowards dare.
they stare,
then cringe
and seek sneaky revenge
as if the blame
for their most precious shortcomings
were someone else's fame
the glitter of which
obscures who is fitter.
machismo,
he always insisted,
was never a matter of
flaunting arrogance
but of overcoming fear
grace under pressure indeed

MISS HOT STUFF

did any dancer
ever dance
more elegantly
than she used to
all but prance
along the sidewalk
her hips swinging
as if to silent fingersnapping singing,
her preemptive back-at-you smile flashing
like the midsummer fountain splashing
in the squirrel tree dappled shade
of old wrought iron mobile's
bienville square?

perhaps not
still she was no wet dream storybook creola
she was only a frisky gal
a wannabe femme fatale

V

GOSPEL REVERBERATIONS

told you once
done told you twice
you'll never get to heaven
shooting dice
ain't no glory
without sacrifice

I looked over my shoulder
and what did I see
a band of red devils with pitchforks
chasing after me

JAWBONE SERMON

Amen brothers and sisters God said
(Amen!)
Said, now Gideon. Said oh Gideon
(Amen!)
Said listen to me Gideon
and hearken to what I'm trying to tell you
(Amen!)
Said I'm trying to tell you something,
   Gideon
(Amen!)
Said I'm trying to tell you something good
for your soul, Gideon
(Amen!)
Said I'm not just concerned with your body
of flesh and blood and sinews and
   sinfulness, Gideon
(Amen—ahah!)

I'm concerned
(ahah!) with your soul, Gideon
(Amen!)

God wants to save our souls brothers and
     sisters
(Amen!)

Said Gideon
(Amen!)
Said you asked me for a sign
(Amen!)
Said I', going to give you a sign Gideon
(Amen!)
Said listen to me Gideon
(Amen!)
I'm going to give you a sign
because you asked me Gideon
(Amen!)

Because I said ask and it shall be given
(oyez!)
I said seek and you shall find.
And I said knock
and the door shall be opened unto you
(Amen!)
Brothers and sisters

unto all men that seek
after goodness and righteousness
(Glory hallelujah!!)
Said *(nahah!)* I'm going to give you a sign
but said *(nahah!)* I want you to trust in me
    too Gideon
(nahah!)
Amen brothers and sisters
said I'm going to give you a sign
because I know how you feel
Said don't think I don't know how you feel
(nahah!)
Because what I asked ain't easy
(Amen!)
Brothers and sisters
don't think God don't know how you feel
all bent down with the troubles of this
    world
But God's ways mysterious
because his will is divine.

Said
amen
Gideon.
Said I might be a jealous God,
but I know how you feel.
Said I might be a wrathful God

but I know how you feel
(*nahah!*)
Believe me I know how you feel.
Said (*nahah!*) yes and I might even be a
    vengeful God,
but that don't mean that I don't know
exactly how you feel.
(*oh yes, amen and amen again!*)
Because am I not also a MERCIFUL God
in all of my almightiness?
Amen!
Brothers and sisters.
Talking about FAITH
(*Glory hallelujah!*)
FAITH

Said Gideon
(*Amen!*)
Didn't I say I would take care of you
if you would only just believe in my holy
    word?
Said didn't I take care of the Hebrew
    children
in a Fiery Furnace
(*nahah!*)
Said (*nahah!*)
didn't I take care of Daniel in a lion's den?

And *(nahah!)*
didn't I take care of Jonah
in the belly of the whale?
And I drowned old Pharaoh's mighty army
    in the Red Sea
to save Moses and the Children of Israel
    (Amen! nahah!)

Said I'm going to give you a sign Gideon
because you got down on your bended
    knee
and asked me
like I myself told you to do
(nahah!)
because I know what you're doubting
is not me and my WORD
and my PROMISE and my GLORY,
    Gideon
but your own self. What you're doubting is
    not
(Amen!)
whether I am the one,
but whether you're the one.
And I understand that.
But
(Glory hallelujah!)
we're talking about FAITH this morning.

Because brothers and sisters,
that's what God ALWAYS talking about.

Said Gideon *(Amen!)*
I'm going to give you the sign
because maybe what you're doubting
is whether or not this is ME.
Said *(Amen!)*
I can understand that too, Gideon
and I'm going to give you a sign
so there can be no doubt about it.
Said I'm going to show you
two signs of the fleece.
And said if you trust in me
I'm going to tell you
how to hand-pick your soldiers
—and you don't need but just a few
as long as you've already got me by your
    side
—and then just to show the world
and confound the nation
I'm going to empower you
to annihilate your foes
and all their multitudes alike
with nothing more than the jawbone of an
    ass!

COLD CLAY CODA FOR OLD MAN
WHICKER BILL COMESAW

will there be any
black brown or yaller folks
at your funeral
and if so
will they be there
to grieve their loss
or to
verify your departure?

ABOUT THE AUTHOR

ALBERT MURRAY was born in Nokomis, Alabama, in 1916. He was educated at Tuskegee Institute, where he later taught literature and directed the college theater. A retired major in the United States Air Force, Murray has been O'Connor Professor of Literature at Colgate University, visiting professor of literature at the University of Massachusetts, writer-in-residence at Emory University, and Paul Anthony Brick Lecturer at the University of Missouri. He is the author of many works of fiction and nonfiction, including the autobiography *South to a Very Old Place,* and the novels *Train Whistle Guitar, The Spyglass Tree,* and *The Seven League Boots.* He lives in New York City.